James H Cousins

**Legend of the Blemished King**

And Other Poems

James H Cousins

**Legend of the Blemished King**
*And Other Poems*

ISBN/EAN: 9783337006020

Printed in Europe, USA, Canada, Australia, Japan

Cover: Foto ©Thomas Meinert / pixelio.de

More available books at **www.hansebooks.com**

THE LITTLE LIBRARY.—VOL. 2.
EDITED BY M. J. KEATS.

# The
# Legend of the
# Blemished King
### And Other Poems.

BY
JAMES H. COUSINS.

WITH COVER DRAWN BY LOUIS H. VICTORY.

Dublin:
BERNARD DOYLE, FRANKLIN PRINTING WORKS,
9 UPPER ORMOND QUAY.
1897.

"Do cum ǵlóiŗe De
aguſ onóŗa na h-éiŗeann,"

AND

TO THE COMPANION OF MY WANDERINGS

AMONG MOST

OF THE SCENES HEREIN MENTIONED,

WHOSE PRESENCE

GILDED THE SUN THAT SHINES UPON,

AND PAINTED THE FLOWERS THAT BEDECK

THE

"FAIR HILLS OF HOLY IRELAND."

# CONTENTS.

|  |  |
|---|---|
| THE LEGEND OF THE BLEMISHED KING— | PAGE |
| PROLOGUE | 19 |
| CANTO I. | 23 |
| CANTO II. | 30 |
| CANTO III. | 37 |
| CANTO IV. | 42 |
| THE LEGEND OF SAINT MAHEE OF ENDRIM | 49 |
| A SONG OF DECADENCE | 65 |
| THE RAILWAY ARCH | 67 |
| SCHAKHE | 70 |
| IN THE GIANT'S RING, BELFAST | 74 |
| THE BLIND FATHER | 78 |
| THE SOUTHERN CROSS | 85 |
| ON THE DEATH OF WILLIAM MORRIS | 87 |
| COPERNICUS | 89 |
| TO ALGERNON CHARLES SWINBURNE | 90 |
| HEAVEN AND EARTH | 91 |
| ON SOME TWENTIETH CENTURY FORECASTS | 92 |
| IRELAND | 93 |

# EDITOR'S NOTE.

Wordsworth, writing a sonnet, having for its subject the sonnet-form, said :—

"To me,
In sundry moods, 'twas pastime to be bound
Within the sonnet's scanty plot of ground;"

and all those who have essayed the task of composing in this particular form will admit that Wordsworth's definition —"scanty plot of ground"—characterises the sonnet's limitations precisely.

As will be observed in the following pages, Mr. Cousins not only excels as a sonneteer; but in "The Legend of the Blemished King" he performs the remarkable feat of producing a poem of classical character, containing forty-eight stanzas, cast perfectly in the no less difficult mould known as the Spenserian stanza—eight heroic lines, followed by an Alexandrine, rhyming thus :—1, 3 ; 2, 4, 5, 7 ; 6, 8, 9.

The subject, however more than the technique, is remarkable. It will have an especial attraction for all who are interested in the ancient literature of Ireland; and, indeed it should be of universal interest, because of the fact that this story of Fergus bears a strong resemblance to the Scriptural narrative of Eden and the Fall of Man. It is a kind of allegory common to all ancient races, containing in its heart an unobtruded moral, wrapped in dramatic incident and decorated with charming pictures of land and sea.

It is, in short, what Fiona M'Leod would call a "legendary morality."

The other poems are equally admirable; and, indeed, however considered, I think that this book should prove a valuable addition to the best literary products of Ireland.

M. J. K.

DEIRDRE.
Illan, what King was he dwelt here of yore?

ILLAN.
Fergus, the son of Leide Lithe-o'-limb,
Ere yet he reigned at Eman, did dwell here.

DEIRDRE.
What, Fergus Wry-mouth? I have heard of him,
And how he came by his ill-favoured name .
Methinks I see him when he rose again
From combat with the monster, and his face,
That had that blemish till love wiped it off,
Serene and ample-featured like a King.

ILLAN.
Not love but anger, made him fight the beast.

DEIRDRE.
No, no, I will not have it anger. Love
Prompts every deed heroic. 'Tis the fault
Of him who did compose the tale at first,
Not to have shown 'twas love unblemished him.

. . . . . .

FERGUS.
All Erin, shore to shore, shall ring with it
And poets in the ages yet to come
Make tales of wonder of it for the world.

"DEIRDRE."—FERGUSON

# The Legend of the Blemished King.

# Prologue: At Scrabo, Co. Down.

*The rugged rock against the sky*
  *Heaves high a tower-topped crest,*
*Whence widens out beneath the eye*
  *The realms of East and West.*
*Here lies a land but seldom sung,—*
  *This crude, majestic crown,*
*And that white sea that moves among*
  *The fertile fields of Down!*

*Unsung!—save when an alien lyre*
  *A moment's space was strung,*
*And Browning fanned a little fire,*
  *And Helen's Tower was sung.*
*Yet storied homes of sept and clan*
  *Are here, and,—dim and vague,—*
*Anear and far, Ben Madighan,*
  *And Keats-sung Ailsa Craig!*

*Unsung !—and wherefore ? lovely land !*
   *Hast thou not ample store*
*For song, from yonder ocean strand,*
   *To Strangford's shining shore ?*
*Hast thou not throbbed to foamy flanks,*
   *And sound of Saxon steel,*
*To crash of Cromwell's rattling ranks,*
   *And Clansmen of O'Neill ?*

*And yet, not all thy songful crown*
   *Is strife of right with wrong ;*
*Here, limpid lark-streams trickle down*
   *A hundred peaks of song ;*
*There, silent sheep and lambkins lie—*
   *A white, uncertain thing—*
*Like lingering snow that fain would spy*
   *The secret of the spring.*

*The roaming robber breezes catch,*
   *And hither upward float,*
*A lusty lilt and vagrant snatch*
   *From some far rustic throat ;*
*And blustering bye, with strident shout,*
   *From scenes of festive glee,*
*That libertine of flower and sprout,*
   *The bacchanalian bee.*

*All life is song :—and song is life*
    *To souls with these akin,*
*Unfettered by yon city's strife,*
    *Unsullied by its sin !*
*Some part of these fair fields and coast,*
    *Some waft of phantom wings,*
*Will haunt my heart, a welcome ghost,*
    *A hint of higher things.*

*Dear land of love and happy lot*
    *Of merry maids and swains,*
*Worthy the martial muse of Scott,*
    *Or Virgil's pastoral strains ;*
*Loved land, this tongue thy song would share*
    *This votive soul is thine :*
*Thy lips are loud with praise and prayer,—*
    *Pray God they kindle mine !*

# The Legend of the Blemished King.

[NOTE :—I am indebted to "The Ecclesiastical History of Down and Connor," by Rev. James O'Laverty, for the story of the "Blemished King." Believing it to be comparatively unknown, and desiring, as far as lay in my power, to spread a knowledge of the interesting stories and legends which abound in Irish History and Literature, I translated it into verse. I learn, however, that a poem on the same subject has been written by the late Sir Samuel Ferguson, under the title of "Fergus Wry-mouth." I can only plead justification for running the inevitable gauntlet of comparison between a giant and a pigmy, on the ground that I had already committed myself to the publication of the present version of the legend before I became aware of the fact mentioned. I have not read the poem by Sir Samuel Ferguson, and I shall not do so until after this volume is in print; but I have written Lady Ferguson on the matter, and she very kindly refuses to see any possible objection to the publication of my rendering of the story, seeing that it contains almost as many stanzas as there are lines in Sir Samuel's.

The Loch of Rory (Ruóṗaıḋe), the centre around which the following story moves, is Dundrum Bay. That bay is still remarkable for its roar, which has been frequently referred to by ancient writers. Even a modern poet (S. K. Cowan, in " Sung by Six ") has written of the bay, " where deep seas moan." Other evidences point to the identity of Rory and Dundrum, in opposition to the conjectures of some that the present Belfast Lough was the scene of the incidents contained in the "Legend of the Blemished King."—THE AUTHOR.]

# CANTO I.

### I.

Eastward in Eireann lay the Lough of Rory.
The Moon, like some pale huntress, landward led
Her white-toothed hounds betwixt the promontory
And its far twin. Thither King Fergus sped
Within his chariot. High his shaggy head
Clove thro' the dusky clouds his chargers made;
And o'er his shoulders, far behind him, spread
Loose locks, and circling cloak, in which arrayed
He, with benignant arm, Ultonia's sceptre swayed.

### II.

Beside him stood his suremost charioteer,
(Muëna, faithful bondsman of his lord,
Favoured in form, and swift of eye and ear),
Urging with well-skilled hand and timely word
The flying steeds. The seaward-soaring bird
Seemed fixed in Heaven, so swift they sped: the day
Lumbered behind, as high the sand they stirred,
And echoes of their wheels that edged the spray
Rolled thro' the silent hills like thunder far away!

## III.

Onward they whirled.  The billows on the beach
  Drew backward in amaze, then, bolder grown,
Sprang forward to the chase, but far from reach
    The phantom bounded on o'er sand and stone;
    Till the low clouds that late-born winds had blown
About the hills, upon the chariot's flight
    Drew down their brows ; or was it they had flown
Thro' dalliant day into a former night
That now, with jealous hand, hid shore and sea from sight ?

## IV.

Then when the day had rallied all its forces,—
  A splash of glory in a murky west,—
Obedient, where it pleased (like men), the horses
    Slackened their speed, and paused, and stood at rest.
    " Thus far, O King ! fulfilled is thy behest,"
Muëna said.  To whom the King : " To thee
    And me 'twere Heaven in Night's soft arms carest
To sleep."—They slept.—Without, that smith, the sea,
On adamantine anvils shaped new shores to be.

## V.

Who knoweth not the spell that lurks in twilight?—
  When mystic murmurs float across the world
From strange, vague forms that hate the brazen highlight
  Of day, and sleep in hidden corners curled
  Till, westward, day has nigh his banner furled.
Then fare they forth : rich spoil, in sooth, they found
  Where Fergus had his mighty figure hurled
Upon the chariot's floor.  They drew around,
Plucked from its sheath his sword, and bore him to the ground,

## VI.

Thence to the verge of ocean.  Fairy elves,
  A thousand strong, the toilsome task essayed ;
While twice a thousand, perched on rocky shelves,
  A wierd accomp'niment of laughter made
  (Timed to their phantom forms that swung and swayed).
So sweet the sound, 'twould seem the winds, at rest
  For once from warring, 'mong the treetops played :
Till, lo, the King, so close they round him prest,
Woke, and a struggling trio clasped upon his breast.

## VII.

"Life for thy life," they cried: "have mercy,
 King!"
Swift to his feet he sprang. The fairy throng
Vanished like vapour, save where, in the ring
 Of his tight-clasping arms, as swift along
 The dim-seen beach he strode the stones among,
The wriggling remnant of the elvish crew
 Craved mercy.—" Mercy doth to thee belong,
And ours in turn to render service due."
Clasping them in his arms he toward his chariot
 drew.


## VIII.

There lay Muëna, wrapt in peaceful sleep,
 Nor woke the King his bondsman; but did say
To those he held his captives: "Through the deep,
 And under, give me knowledge of the way,
 Unfearful of the power of wave or spray.
This shall ye grant and live." "O King, such
 boon,"
 Thus said the elves, "sweeps not beyond our
 sway;
So shall be thine, ere swings another moon,
Skill meet to dare the depths of river and lagoon,

## IX.

"Save Rory, whence thou camest; that shalt thou
  Ne'er ruffle with thy foot : within its wide
Impassioned breast, from day's first dawn till now,
  And still from now till dawn's last day, has plied,
  And still shall ply, the spirit of the tide
His secret craft.  Nor thou nor human kind
  Shall scan his face and live.  All else beside
Is thine when Earth 's again to Day resigned,
Whose advent now is blown on trumpets of the wind."

## X.

So when the morn, like Virtue's cheek red-blushing
  For night's black deeds, from couch of cloud arose,
Ere yet were heard hoarse caws and dark wings rushing
  Athwart the sun, when trailing lines of crows
  Hasten to haunts far off that no man knows,
Beside the sea stood King and charioteer
  To take the waves' great secret now from those
In promise bound, who stand apart, yet near,
Where wavelets lift and lay, as if some word to hear.

## XI.

Then spake the first of fairies : " O great King,
　　Thy life was ours—we spared it; ours was thine
And thou didst spare us, yet encompassing
　　Thy deed with obligation, line on line,
　　And promise holding promise,—me and mine
To do, and thou to do not.　Now the hour
　　Hath come—as ne'er before—when billow and brine
Yield to a mortal every whit of power—
Save one—how suns soe'er may shine or clouds may lower."

## XII.

Low bowed the Monarch his assenting head.
　　The elfin chieftain swiftly drew anear
Doffing his hood, long-trailing, ruby red.
　　Lo! on the King 'tis placed.　In either ear
　　They plant sweet spices, herbs, anointing clear;
And weird enchantments drown the muffled roar
　　Of throbbing ocean.　Then the charioteer
Beholds his master pass the waters o'er,
And stands, a lonely man upon a lonely shore.

　　　　．　　．　　．　　．　　．　　．

## XIII.

Day brightened in the East, and o'er the waters
  The round sun rose and threw across the wave
A lambent flame, blood-red, as though from slaughters
  In Orient lands. The breaking surf did lave
  Muëna's feet: he, wrapt in wonderings grave,
Looked long and wistful, such as lovers do
  To greet their love. At length the wondering slave
Saw on the deep a form that neared, and grew,
And stepped upon the beach—the King returned anew.

## CANTO II.

### XIV.

Thenceforth, King Fergus, strong in power new born,
   Recked not a restful hour, but, passion-fired,
And strong in strength un'customed, night and morn
   Probed to the farthest deeps his soul desired.
   At such swift speed too soon his soul acquired
The sum of knowledge granted. "All below,"
   So spake the King, "to which I have aspired
Is mine,—that earth or ocean can bestow,
Save one, whose secret fain my mind would grasp and know."

### XV.

So chafe Restriction's fetters. So within
   Dwelleth for ever ancient Adam's will.
Sweet though the tasted fruit, the fruit unseen,
   Or seen but yet forbid, is sweeter still.
   Lord of the land, of river, vale, and hill,
King Fergus stood, and "Wherefore," thus said he,
   "This circumscription? What of greater ill
Dwelleth within the breast of mine own sea
Than those whose farthest caves have felt the foot of me?

## XVI.

"I *will* descend to Rory: haply there
   May dwell some secret whose resistless charm,
Bent to my kindred's service, danger, care
   Shall put apart, and shield from hurt or harm
   In council grave or battle's loud alarm.
What ho, Muëna. Haste my charioteer.
   Who boasts that weak has grown my kingly arm
To sweep its path of all restriction clear?
Fergus is Fergus still—and Fergus knows no
   fear!"


## XVII.

Muëna heard, and answered word by deed.
   Soon rolled the chariot round the palace hall,
And Eastward toward the ocean; steed by steed
   Stretched to the task his limbs; their hoofs did
     fall
   Like rain on summer noons. The curlews' call
Gave token of the near-approaching end,
   And soon before their eyes the ocean wall
Shouldered the shock of waters that extend
To meet the sky. The King did to the marge
   descend.

## XVIII.

Know you the Loch of Rory? Sages tell
　How, when the sons of Adam felt the force
Of watery judgments, came a vagrant swell
　And burst round shores of Eireann. Man and horse,
King, chief, and clansman, in the widening course
Of high, resistless billows, sank from sight
　'Mong cries from throats in sudden anguish hoarse
That called, and called, and ceased when fell the night,—
And on a stranger shore soft broke the morning's light.

## XIX.

Across this shore Ultonia's King now passed.
　The waves that rattled up the pebbled strand
Rose in their ranks, then low before him cast
　Themselves, and stood aside on either hand.
　The King moved forward. Never magic wand
More swift compelled submission. Thro' the spray,
　As tho' he trod upon the level land,
He took, 'twixt watery walls, a deepening way,
Till o'er his head the waves shut out the light of day.

## XX.

Forward he fared.  No swimmer's opened eye
  E'er scanned so sweet a sight.  In glimmering green
Slow lightening upward to the watery sky
  That arched the watery world, in softer sheen
  Than mortals wot of, lay the fairy scene :—
Fantastic rocks, sea-flowers that rose and fell
  As brushed by silent shapes that moved between
Him and the darkening distance, fairy cell,
And beds of ocean bloom more sweet than Asphodel.


## XXI.

There sat the King adown to scan the world
  Of more than wonder.  Thither came to sue
For explanation things that swam, and curled,
  Then circled round, and passed away from view.
  Here stood as 'twere a camp, and there a few
Forms, not of ocean, human arms outspread.
  King Fergus wept to make the sad review
Where those who faced the flood, now dumb and dead,
Slept out the tale of time upon the ocean's bed.

## XXII.

Short space he sat when, from athwart the deep,
  There came a sound of horror ! Far and near
A wild commotion rose, as things that creep,
  Or climb, or swim, smitten with sudden fear,
  Darkened the depths that erst had been so clear.
King Fergus started upward to his feet,
  And saw, but dimly, toward him quickly steer
A dreadful shape that came like lightning fleet,
And chilled the monarch's blood such fearful foe to meet.

## XXIII.

It was the Muirdris!! Nought that men have known
  Could match its awful visage : high upheld
On ogrish limbs, one moment ape-like grown,
  It flew along, till, lo! it sank, and swelled
  To size gigantic, while it yelped and yelled
In sound that spake of fury, fiendish ire.
  In tremulous awe the King the beast beheld
Bent in its course on devastation dire,
While from its eyeballs streamed malignant lines of fire.

## XXIV.

Round turned the King, and flew as 'twere from Death!
Swift sped the beast within his foamy track.
Wreathed round his form the King could feel its breath,
Nor dared he glance one smallest moment back.
Behind the twain, like tempest-driven rack,
Spread clouds of foam, pointing the path of each.
Above, white billows lashed the shore. His neck
Muëna, wondering, strained,—till on the beach
Swooned the swift-fleeing King beyond the monster's reach.

## XXV.

But tho' Muëna wondered as he saw
His King, 'mid foamy spray, make sudden flight,
Far more he wondered as he scanned the flaw
Upon the King's wan face, that made the sight
More dreadful than some horror-haunted night.
Lo! wide apart, and stretched from ear to ear,
In sudden aspect of tremendous fright,
Gaped, like a cave, his jaws: the eyes, once clear,
Stared as upon a sight of overmastering fear.

## XXVI.

Muëna bore the King upon his breast
    Into the chariot.  There he laid him, dazed,
On ample couch, his fevered form to rest,
    Soft shaded from the sun, that burned and blazed
    High overhead,—then whipt the steeds, as crazed
From some pursuing phantom.  Might and main
    In lightning alternation high they raised
Sure-stepping foot, and over hill and plain
Toward far Emania's walls their swiftest strength they strain.

# CANTO III.

## XXVII.

Not far the sun had fallen, when he drew
  The chargers' reins beside the circling sweep
Of Royal walls.  The gathering clansmen knew
  From foam and steam no slow and leisured creep
  Had been their pace.  Their thought took leap on leap
From sight to meaning.  Then upon the floor
  They spied the King recumbent as in sleep,
And as the form was borne within the door,
In others' eyes they sought the secret o'er and o'er.

## XXVIII.

Straightway into the council-room of chiefs
  And sages was the limp-limbed body borne.
Then spake Muëna : " Lo ! a grief of griefs,
  Ultonia's hearts are kingless and forlorn,
  For know ye not how spake the wiseman, born
To wisdom ?—' Ne'er shall King with blemish marred
  Reign ' : and behold ! alas ! since this sad morn
King Fergus, from Ambition evil-starred,
Lies now before your eyes in visage sorely scarred.

## XXIX.

" Choose ye a King, to reign within his stead."
He ceased, but answer came not; rather, round
The silent throng flew questioning glance that said
   Unstable vacillation. Not a sound
   Broke cover till one bolder spirit wound
The trumpet-horn of speech ; then left and right,
   Leapt forth the hounds of thought, and roof and ground
Echoed impassioned tongues, and feet bedight
With thong and sandal, plied with each loud speaker's might.


## XXX.

Then spake the sons of wisdom, they who stood
   Apart in silent conclave, while the din
Of ineffectual babblings drew no rood
   More near conclusion : " Hear, Ultonian kin !
   What arm so strong Ultonia's wars to win,
Foster the strength of strong, inspire the weak ?
   Lives there a soul full fit to stand within
The Monarch's room ? What worthier do you seek
To guide the reins of peace, or would ye other ? Speak ! "

## XXXI.

" None ! none !" the multitudinous answer rang
  Unanimous.  (King Fergus, with a sigh,
Turned in his sleep.  Perchance he dreamed there sang
  Some bard of deeds their fathers did.)  The cry
  Thrilled through the chamber's walls, and far and nigh
Found answer in a thousand throats, that gave
  Their yet unmeaning plaudits to the sky ;
And as, in sound like shoreward-shrieking wave
They shout, the secret they in others' faces crave.

## XXXII.

Without, the crowd swayed back and forth, with din
  Low-muffled, as the sea doth surge and sway
In silken swell, from storm gone past.  Within
  Was calm, and brows determined sought a way
  Through that old law to write emphatic "Nay!"
Then quoth the wisemen's chief : " Our path is plain.
  Our hearts upon our tongues have said their say,
And Fergus o'er Ultonia's host shall reign,
If but to meet our thoughts your constant strength ye strain.

## XXXIII.

" Let fools and babblers take their journey far,
  And silent sit as sent'nel to your speech.
What wots the King of that which him doth mar
  If but the knowledge in the breast of each
    Be locked beyond a thought's long-arméd reach
Till forced forgetfulness doth rust the key
  Or haply lose it. E'en your art let teach
The water to forget his form to see
Or give it back, when to ablution cometh he."


## XXXIV.

Approval shone within their eyes. Their tongues
  In loud assent gave forth: " Fergus is King!"
And once again without, untutored lungs
  Caught up the cry, nor knew what meant the thing,
'Till, like a mighty bird, on fresh-plumed wing,
The Royal chariot once again did shake
  Rampart and roof, as champing steeds did fling
Their heads on high, and sped by mount and brake
To scenes of less surprise when Fergus should awake.

   .   .   .   .   .   .

## XXXV.

What need to sing of deeds within the scope
   Of thrice a dozen moons? What need to tell
How fared the King when, by the sanded slope
   Where twice a day the sea-waves fret and swell,
He woke? Or devious deeds that oft befell
Clansman and chief in those high-sounding days
   Of war-girt peace—a Heaven ringed round with Hell—
Or battle's loud-lunged shout, or conquest's blaze,
Or how the blemished King ne'er on his fault did gaze.

# CANTO IV.

### XXXVI.

'Twas thus—and thus, when thrice a year had sped
    King Fergus of his blemish happed to know:—
" I go to mine ablutions (so he said
    Unto his bond-maid), girl, the task you know
    Of preparation. Haste you, for I go
On mighty mission!" P'r'aps 'twas Fate's decree
    The maiden's arm in service seemed full slow,
And Fergus, strained of nerve, was swift to see
In microscopic faults, some slight of majesty.


### XXXVII.

Howbeit,—the fire to firelike will give blaze,
    And progeny of one small word or deed
Count thousand-thousand. Half in wide amaze,
    And half in wild vexation that slow heed
    The maiden gave to that his will decreed,
He strode into her presence : then on high
    He raised the stinging lash his stout-skinned steed
Oft felt, and flinched, and, drawing swiftly nigh,
Its serpent hiss was drowned in the smit' maiden's cry.

## XXXVIII.

"A curse upon your laggard form!" he hissed.
  The smitten girl swift raised her flashing eyes
In scarlet indignation, nor was missed
  The blemish on the Monarch's face. She cries:
  " King Fergus, heartless coward! I loathe, despise
Your craven hand, nor e'en a word would deign,
  But that I deem your spirit's shape and size
Must match your brute-like visage." Purpling plain
With rage, he drew his sword and cut the maid in twain.

## XXXIX.

A maddened moment's deed! And when the storm
  Was past, the King in calm the wreck surveyed
Of his own making. Towering o'er the form
  Prostrate and purple, holding still the blade
  Wet with her life, he stood as sore dismayed,
Muttering: "Visage! Visage!" still the word
  Beat inward on his 'wildered brain, nor stayed
Till that grim truth, long hid, to sight restored,
Burst on his mind. He turned, still clasping tight the sword.

## XL.

Three steps beyond the portal of the room
  Where lay the maid, he stopped and cast a look
Backward,—a look portentous of dark doom
  To all beneath its ban.  Aloft he shook
  The bleeding blade; then cried, till every nook,
E'en to the farthest of the farthest halls,
  Trembled; and, as he called, his way he took
Down corridors that held his foot's swift falls
Till cry and footfall blent without the castle walls.

## XLI.

The cry was: "Visage! Visage! Death and blood
  To what has wrought the ruin of yon maid,—
That hideous habitant of Rory's flood
  Who plies—mayhap not long—his secret trade;
  And mine ambition that such depths essayed
As strained the strength of me.  Yet, not for nought
  The fiend was found, tho' fled I sore dismayed:
Some lesson yet is there, tho' anguish-taught;
Some profit yet remains, tho' it in blood be bought.

## XLII.

One falleth—that foul spirit: then is past
   Temptation of ambition; but, perchance
Mine arm may fail: sobeit, then is cast
   Away the secret." On did he advance.
   And one who saw his eyeballs' lightning glance,
And marked his mood and manner, thro' the crowd
   Spread rumouring words, keen, swift as strong-threwn lance,
That drew them forth, a multitude, all browed
With wonderment that grew with each swift stride, till, loud

## XLIII.

And deep before them, Rory swells and swings.
   Behold! the King nor pauses, nor aside
Turns in his track.—Not mine to tell of things
   Run riot in those minds that edged the tide,
   Where late the billows did King Fergus hide,
Nor gave of him a token, save the swell
   Of giant strivings in the waters wide,
And one wild wave that, as from heart of Hell,
Leaped for the shore and 'mong the wondering warriors fell.

## XLIV.

And thereupon arose confusion, such
  As ne'er was seen before, and ne'er again
Shall e'er be seen.  With tops that seemed to touch
  The heights of Heaven arose the strenuous main
  In wild tumultuous strivings, till the brain
Of those beholders whirled, and they that spake
  In terror seemed all voiceless, for in vain
Speech called at its own ears.  All heaven did make
Sound at whose dreadful voice all earth did seem to shake.

## XLV.

And far across the world a tempest bore
  Sounds of a conflict such as never yet
Man's eyes beheld,—e'en to the cloudy shore
  Of distant Britain : there did they beget
  Vague words of wonder.  Ere the sun had set
Within a stormy west nor man nor maid
  Of all Ultonia but with spray was wet
As, lo! from each far hill, each distant glade
Long thousands shoreward drew with wide-eyed wonder swayed.

## XLVI.

And when it seemed as if the heavens swam
  In wild bewilderment,—each starry sphere
Would topple earthward, straightway fell a calm
  That laid a hush upon the heart of fear,
  And soothed both sea and sky, till softest tear
Would drop with sound of cataracts in the glen.
  And thus they waited what should next appear,
Uncounted thousands of full-armëd men,
Bards, chieftans, clansmen, women, maids, youths,
  children:—then

## XLVII.

As if the sea had stolen half the glow
  Of the sunk sun, the quiet Loch flushed red,
And lengthened day, e'en tho' the day did go
  To other lands. "Some portent this," they said,
  "Of the fight's finish: one hath joined the dead—
Which, shall appear full soon."—Lo! on the sea
  What form is yon that waves a hideous head
Within its hand? They gaze, they shout: "'Tis he,
Fergus, Ultonia's King. Fergus hath victory!"

## XLVIII.

Then that red glory brightened, and they scanned
   The King's marred visage—marred?—nay, pure and bright
As erst in youth! He called: "With this right hand
   Nerved with the fury of revengeful might,
I fought—and won! I've lived my day; now night
Doth wrap its blackness round me: I but pay
   The price of mine own deed." And from their sight
He sank beneath the waters of the bay
Which rolled in waves of blood for many a devious day!

# The Legend of St. Mahee of Endrim.

# The Legend of Saint Mahee of Endrim.

## To J. A. Gregg.

[Note.—Saint Mahee (moċaoı) was born about 420 A.D., founded the Abbey of Endrim (Oenopuim—the single ridge), on the beautiful island bearing that name, about 450, and died in the year 496 or 497. For several centuries the Abbey, in which education and religion were combined, occupied a prominent position, and turned out a number of subsequent founders of similar institutions. Between 974 and 1178 history is silent in regard to it, but it is certain that, from its position on Cuan (Cuan—a lough, now Strangford), which was infested by Danish marauders, it came in for a large share of their devastating attentions. From the date of its affiliation with an English educational establishment, 1178, it seems to have fallen on evil days, and in 1450 it is simply noted as a Parish Church in the charge of the Bishop of Down.

The Island of Endrim—or, as it is now called, in memory of its Patron Saint, Mahee—is situated most picturesquely on Strangford Lough, about seven miles from Comber, Co. Down, and is approachable on foot or car by a modern causeway-road, which crosses an intervening island. On the shoreward end of the island may be seen many remnants of the stone buildings which superseded the original wooden structures. These remnants include the stump of a round tower; traces of extensive foundations once laid bare by the late Bishop Reeves, but now almost entirely hidden from view; the site of the harbour where anchored "ships from Britain;" evidences of a hallowed God's-acre, and a fairly complete castle of a later period. The circuit of the island can be made on foot leisurely in a couple of hours, and the walk affords a view of the extensive waters of the once Dane-infested lough, the distant hoary walls of Greyabbey, the haunts of Saint Patrick, the reputed scene of the death of Ollav Fola (oLLaṁḃ ḟoóla, the lawgiver of Erin), and the martial deeds of De Courcey.

Ballydrain, about half-way between Comber and Mahee Island, is so-called from baıle, a townland, and ɒṗaıṡın, a blackthorn tree; and the reader will observe the connection between this place and the Island of Mahee. No trace of a church has yet been discovered at Ballydrain.

The idea contained in the Legend has been variously rendered by several eminent authors. The incident in which it is here embodied may, however, be fairly claimed as the oldest version—the original, in fact.—THE AUTHOR.]

---

Lo! right and left, in calm repose,
    Are spread unnumbered isles,
Between whose shores the bluff breeze blows,
    And sungilt Strangford smiles.
The shoreward way our feet have left
    Below, still winds along
Where strenuous waves, in eddy and cleft,
    Croon low their iterant song.

II.

Bright in the passionate, tremulous rays
    From cloudy towers of day,
Yon crumbling castle seems to gaze
    At castles far away,
Like parted friends of other years
    Who meet, nor waste a word,
But wondering stand, and smile thro' tears
    From depths unfathomed stirred.

### III.

Here may we rest, and make our seat
    On this high rock-strewn mound,
" Put off our shoes from off our feet "—
    We tread on holy ground;
The haunts where many a sandalled sole
    Trod out life's lust and woe,
And, stedfast set to one high goal,
    Went down in dust below.

### IV.

No stone is theirs engraven large
    With record born of strife,
No gilded scroll, no carven marge,
    No legend loud with life.
Far other deeds than men applaud
    Their holy hands essayed,
In life viceregent here of God,
    In death still undismayed.

### V.

No fluctuant favours—servile spouse
    Of princes' transient smile—
Did e'er bedeck their sacred brows,
    Their saintly souls defile:
No life-warm lips their own had kissed
    (Earth's hope-inspiring dove)—
Their life was one long Eucharist
    Eternalised in love.

## VI.

The workers went ; the works remain.
    Time here small kingship owns.
Thro' 'whelming winds, thro' sun and rain,
    Have lived these lichened stones,
And that brief tower upreared by those
    Whose dread was from the deep,—
In strife their strength, in peace repose,
    Their guardian now in sleep.

## VII.

Thine eyes, old tower, have scanned the scroll
    And palimpsest of Earth,
And fain would we thy thoughts unroll
    Thro' years of bliss or dearth,
For thou from thy calm height dost look
    With sage, dispassionate eye,
To where the star of day-dawn shook
    Within a youthful sky.

## VIII.

We deem thee old ; but age is not
    A toll of hours and days,—
Mean measure of our little lot
    And arbitrary ways.
We run our little round of change
    Thro' years of less or more,
But Time to thee holds nought of strange,
    Unheard, unseen before.

## IX.

Down paths of night no starrier balls
    No new Milanion throws ;
Thro' no transfigured day's high halls
    Th' itinerant breeze still blows;
Belligerent ever, baffled still,
    Th' importunate surges swing ;
Still dear as dawn th' ecstatic thrill
    And prophet power of Spring.

## X.

Wrapt in a dream of ancient days
    Thou stand'st aloof from ours,
Yet nought hast thou of battle's blaze
    Or blighting iron showers ;
For well-beloved art thou of moon,
    And sun, and winds, and stars,
Forever in thy heart attune
    To every statelier bars

## XI.

Than aught my highest hope could know
    In this inspiring breath
Where wilding blossoms bloom and blow,
    As life blooms out of death ;
Yet fain, withal, my lips would wed
    To song, for modern ears,
This chord from lyric days long dead,
    This dream from epic years:

## The Legend.

Quoth good Saint Mahee of Endrim,
    "I shall build for Christ my master
Here a church, and here defend him
    And His cause from all disaster."
Seven score youths cut beam and wattle,
Seven score hands unseared in battle
    Their unstinted aid did lend him,
        Fast and ever faster.

But tho' arm, and voice loud-ringing,
    To a test of toil defied him,
Right and left the wattles flinging,
    Not a tongue could dare deride him;
For, before them all, he stood
Finished, waiting. Not a rood
    From the spot a bird was singing
        In a thorn beside him.

Sang no bird in ancient story
    Half so sweet or loud a strain :
Seaward to the Lough of Rory,
    Landward then, and back again,
Swelled the song, and trilled and trembled
O'er the toiling youths assembled,
    Rang around 'mid Summer glory
        There at Ballydrain.

Far more beautiful the bird was
    Than the bright-plumed Bird of Bliss
And the Abbot's feeling stirred was
    To its deepest depths, I wis;
'Till, as from the fiery splendour
Moses saw, in accents tender
    Spake the bird, and lo, the word was:
        " Goodly work is this ! "


" True," quoth Saint Mahee of Endrim,
    " 'Tis required by Christ my master
Here to build, and here defend Him
    And His cause from all disaster;
But my blood mounts high with weening
Of this goodly word the meaning ? "
    Nearer then the bird did tend him,
        Fast and even faster.


" I shall answer. I descended
    From mine angel-soul's compeers,
From my home serene and splendid
    To this haunt of toil and tears;
Came to cheer thee with a note
From an angel's silvern throat."
    Then he sang three songs: each, ended,
        Made a hundred years.

There, thro' days that dawned and darkened,
    With his wattles by his side,
Stood the island Saint and hearkened
    To that silvery-flowing tide;
Stood entranced, and ever wond'réd,
Till had circled thrice a hundred
    Years o'er fields, life-lade or stark, and
    Strangford's waters wide.


Then when came the final number,
    Ceased the angel-bird its strain,
And, unheld by ills that cumber
    Mortals, sought the heavenly plain.
Then the Saint, in mute amaze,
Round him turned an anxious gaze,
    And from that far land of slumber
    Came to Earth again.


Low his load, mid weed and flower,
    Lay beside him all unbroken,
Till, with thrice augmented power,
    From his holy dream awoken,
Up he bore it to his shoulder,—
Broad and not a hand's breath older.
    Scarce, thought he, had passed an hour
    Since the bird had spoken.

Toward his island church he bore it.
  Lo, an oratory gleaming,
And "To Saint Mahee," writ o'er it!
  "Now," quoth he, "in faith I'm dreaming!
Say, good monk, at whose consistory
Shall I solve this mighty mystery,
  And to form of fact restore it
    From this shadowy seeming?"


Thus he spake to one who faced him
  With a look of mild surprise,
One who swiftly brought and placed him
  'Neath the Abbot's searching eyes.—
Leave him there: not mine to rhyme of
Deeds that filled the latter time of
  Him who, fain tho' years would waste him,
    Ages not, nor dies.

. . . . . . . . . .

Such the wondrous old-time story
  Of the bird's long, lethal strain
Sung thro' Summers hot and hoary,
  Winters white on mount and main
And the monks, to mark the mission
Of the bird,—so tells tradition,—
  Built a church to God's great glory
    There at Ballydrain.

### XII.

The song has ceased, the dream is done,
    Lo, nought but shattered shrine
And weed-clad walls greet now the sun
    That sparkles in the brine;
Yet these no remnant are of dead
    Insalutary days,
Vicarious blood of morning, shed
    For more than Memphian haze.

### XIII.

The fires of worship, and of war,
    De Courcey's marshalled hosts,
The rude sea-rovers from afar
    Have vanished from our coasts;
And out of these an ampler field
    Found Freedom, mind and hand,
Toward unattempted ends to wield
    A world-enchanting wand.

### XIV.

What tho' in oft ignoble cause
    The wave of war still rolls,
The hate of sects, the clutching claws,
    The strife of armoured souls;
What tho' the thousands, born to fail,
    In darkness come and go,
Be ours no pessimistic wail
    Of fear for larger woe;

## XV.

For even now the dawn doth give
  Some promissory gleams,
Tho' most 'tis ours in night to live,
  Participant in dreams
Of some broad-beamed and brighter morn,
  Some elemental balm,
Some purer peace, of battle born,
  Some tempest-cradled calm!

# Miscellaneous Poems.

## A Song of Decadence.

I wonder if there still remain
    Some echoes from the songs of old;
Or what the measure of the strain
    The future shall unfold?

The voice that breathed across the years,
    And came, and went, and passed the bar,
And sang the battle song of tears,
    Sounds small, and faint, and far;

And men have found another chord,
    An offspring, not of heart, but head;
And gold is God, and lust is Lord,
    And Love lies stricken dead!

Ah, me! the race goes blindly on
    And leaves the old familiar ways;
And still, earth-weighted, flowers the dawn
    To still ignoble days;

And men, as sheep within their folds,
    Grope round their world with great sad eyes;
And hate the hand that still withholds
    The secret of the skies;

Or, deeming God an idle tale
  Withdrawn from lore of ancient shelves,
Themselves would reckon by the scale
  And measure of themselves!

How mean the stature of the song
  Of our inglorious—glorious time,
Attenuating, as along
  It moves from that great prime

When Milton, in the midnight hours,
  Lay waiting for the mystic breath
Of God to touch his soul to flowers
  Of song that smile at Death.

O singers of the years to come!
  Be yours the large and liberal scope:
Sing sweetly—or for aye be dumb—
  Of God, and Love, and Hope,

Encircled by no little line
  Of gain or loss, of time or sense,
Nor, bent at Mammon's soulless shrine,
  Your birth-right part for pence;

But bend an arm across the past,
  And finger all the vibrant years,
Till sunlight, on our shadows cast,
  Makes rainbows of our tears.

## The Railway Arch.

There it stands, as it has stood—
   Theme for bards, and theme for seers—
Mute to sun and tempests rude,
   To the swift express of years;

Stretched across from bank to bank
   Where the rabbits flash and go,
Where the fir-trees, rank by rank,
   Gaze upon the track below

As the train, at man's behest,
   In the calm or tempest's teeth,
Speeds with lightning in its breast,
   And the thunder underneath.

There in many a rift and rent,
   Many a bird finds friendly cover;
And the toiler, homeward bent,
   Whistles as he passes over;

And the children from the town
   Climb its parapets and strain
Half a hundred throats to drown
   With a cheer the passing train.

Yet how many children, toilers,
   List' to what that arch would say
To the thousands of earth's moilers ?—
   Dull of ear and listless they !

Ah ! adown the track of time,
   In the world's great sidings lying,
Many a theme for many a rhyme
   Is unmarked by thousands, flying

After all the fen-fires, darting
   In the damps and swamps of life ;
Fires of meeting and of parting,
   Hate and love, and strain and strife !

There it stands—O ! how I love it ;
   For it speaks of weal, and woe,
For the thousands pass above it ;
   For the thousands rush below ;

And, attune to whirr and clatter,
   Wide and wider does it span,
High o'er time and sense and matter,
   High o'er life and death and man,

Stretched from age to age unborn ;
   And above it in a stream
Pass, unceasing, night and morn,
   Shapes like those in Jacob's dream

All the souls of all the ages,
    All the ghosts of all the years,
Priests and prophets, saints and sages,
    Sweet-breathed bards and broad-browed
        seers,

Who from many a cloudy station
    List' the whirring of the wheels
Bounding on without cessation,
    Dragging progress at their heels;

Who, as children from the town,
    Throng the parapets, and strain
Form and voice in flashing down
    Warning signals to the train

Speeding on, at man's behest,
    In the calm, or tempest's teeth,
With the lightning in its breast,
    And the thunder underneath!

# Schakhe.

(A Ballad of Armenia.)

They had fought, they had failed, those women;
   and now, in a wild-eyed throng,
They fled from the red destroyer, and they cried:
   " O Lord, how long?—
How long, O Lord, till the ending of the ghastly
   sounds and sights,
Till the dripping days be finished, and the thrice
   red-running nights,—
Till the last cold corpse falls, severed from the last
   Armenian head,
Till the last maid be dishonoured, and the last hot
   tear be shed? "

They had fled from the red destroyer, but he
   hastens around their track,
Till the fate they had flown is before them, and
   they turn in their pathway back.
But, Northward and Southward and Eastward and
   Westward, and round and round,
Come the gleam of the steely lightning, and the
   wild, soul-harrowing sound,

As mother and sister and daughter, and the child at its mother's breast
Go down in the surge of slaughter and the wreck of the great Opprest.
And now they are huddled together, as the death-cries rise and swell,
Where the rock runs up to Heaven, and the gulf goes down to Hell,—
On the edge of a beetling hillock ; when, lo ! from the 'wildered crowd,
On a peak of the rock steps Schakhe, and calls to her sisters, loud :—


"O sisters in nameless sorrow, baptised in a life of tears ;
Before you two paths lie open : behind you a thousand years
Fade far in the dusky distance, one long, broad stream of blood,
That flows by the wreck and ruin of sword and fire and flood !
Before you two paths lie open : one leads where dangers lurk,
And the pain and the dumb dishonour from the merciless hand of the Turk.

Choose ye ! Will ye thread that pathway, prove
false to the men ye love ;
Prove false to the children ye bore them ; prove
false to the God above ?
Will ye sell yourselves to the spoilers of father
and mother and child,
Who butchered and then, like devils, at their
cries for mercy smiled ?
Do ye think of the thousands rotting, flung down
in a ghastly heap
Unblessed ; whose dust commingles in their last
unhallowed sleep ?
Do ye think of the blood, the sorrow, the wild,
sky-rending cries,
As the scarce-born babe was mangled to feast
their fiendish eyes ?
Do you think of the brute defilement when, full in
the flare of day,
Ye were robbed of your dear-prized honour, and
made the Moselm's prey ?
Will ye choose that path, O sisters ? 'Tis a path
ye have often trod ;
Or throw yourselves on the mercy of the great, all-
powerful God ?

What though He is veiled in silence, and behind our clouds grown dim;
If He come not down to help us, then we will go to Him.
See! there is the other pathway, down, down to the home of Night.
Jump! long ere the body be broken, the soul will have taken flight.
He will give His charge to His angels: in their hands they will bear thee up,
As ye tread the Saviour's pathway, and drink the Saviour's cup.
There,—lean on my breast, sweet infant, and good-bye to Earth and woe.
Now, sisters, the way lies open: I am weary and long to go!"

They had fought: they had failed; and they followed brave Schakhe, a martyr throng;—
And soft o'er the corpse-strewn valley the winds sigh: "Lord, how long?"

## In the Giant's Ring, Belfast.

No Shakespeare girdle this, whose girth
    Would compass with its arms
The sounding seas and snows of earth,
    The fruitful fields and farms.*
Here priestly power has thrown around
    A circuit wide and high,
A bar where waves of human sound
    Beat vainly, drop, and die.

" Who dreams of war in such a scene
    Of undisturbed repose?
Who babbles here of spite and spleen?
    Who rhymes of human woes?
Nought here is heard of mingling cries,
    Of life's unlovely jars;
Nought here is seen but yonder skies,
    And circling suns and stars!"

O wise in wisdom of the fool!
    O warped in sight and soul!
O Arctic spirit, icy cool
    As passions of the Pole!

---

\* . . . . Put a Girdle round the earth
    In forty minutes.

Is 't but a dream of babe or bard
   That conjures grief and groans ?
Or is thy shrunken heart more hard
   Than those three standing stones ?

I dreamed a dream when last I stood
   Within their sombre shade :
Time took my hand full many a rood
   Beyond the tides of trade,
Beyond the sacerdotal rite,
   And soul-absorbing creeds,
Beyond the narrow skirts of sight
   And despicable deeds.

I soared above the brimming Earth ;
   I peered beneath its breast ;
I saw the founts of joy and mirth,
   And seats of life's unrest.
But in the ocean of its thought
   One current swelled and grew
And on to seas with blessing fraught
   A thousand others drew.

'Twas Love: and Time stood by, and said :
   " Behold ! a thousand spires
Speak gilded words from hearts as dead
   As those old Druid fires.

But love lives on and leavens all
   In Earth's expanding range,
The height and depth, the rise and fall,
   The first and last of Change.

" Kings pale and perish, dogmas die,
   The world goes slowly on
To greet an all-unclouded sky,
   To kiss a purer dawn.
Stript of the garb of mimic worth,
   Freed from his brothers' ban
And circumscribing creeds, steps forth
   A newer, nobler man.

" 'Twas thus God's chosen race was bent
   Beneath a tyrant yoke :
'Twas thus the hated chains were rent,
   The conqueror's sceptre broke.
Thus Babylon to Persia bowed,
   Thus Persia bent to Greece,
Thus Greece gave place to Rome the proud,
   The Goth broke Roman peace."

These mighty stones, this giant ring
   Give token of a day
That died, as dies a dreamt-of thing,
   And passed in dust away,

Save these, for you—dear heart—and me
   To gaze on, muse, and rhyme :
"Time conquers all, both bond and free,
   But Love shall conquer Time!"

## The Blind Father.

### I.

So, my son, you came this morning at the blinking of the day,
"King, and heir for Uther," riding swiftly shoreward on the spray
That, within my face, comes blowing from a stranger sea and sky,—
Felt, not seen—upon whose margin here, a sightless Merlin, I
Stand, and turn my head and harken to the whisper of the wind
Borne from seaward on to leeward,—dark before and dark behind.

### II.

And they say you're like your father?—How can I know, for I look
With a dead eye into darkness; yet I've felt upon a book
Something tell me: "In His form and with His likeness made He man:"
So you're like your father, and he looks like God—but, ah! the ban,

A Damocles-blade, keeps hanging, as o'er ancient
  Adam's head,
O'er last moment's latest Adam, just arisen from
  the dead.

### III.

Ban! Who banned you? Is it God, or is it man
  suspends the knife?
God decreed you'd toil for bread, but man decrees
  you'll die for life!

### IV.

"From the dead."—You like the phrase not, wife;
  yet not from death he's come,
But from life, of all the ages past the product and
  the sum.
Thine and mine,—yet neither mine nor thine, but
  heir of every hour,
Drawing through thee from the world's breast,—
  we the stem and he the flower.
Ours, and yet not ours; the acorn from its parent
  will be broke,
Drop to earth, from earth to heaven stretch the
  fingers of the oak.
Acorn—oak, and back to acorn, hedging all the
  hills of time,
On and on forever, housing birds of every wing
  and clime.

Thus we die,—and thus we die not; mortal, yet immortal we;
Closely clasping crumbling fingers round the hand of the To Be;
Flingling out along the ages tendrils that will grip, and twine
In a slow attenuation down the long posterior line.

V.

Thus the generations, marching to an universal strain,
Start, and stop; and in the starting from Da Capo sing again.

VI.

Ah! not ours: yet ours the moulding of a future near or far;
Ours to set a sun in heaven,—hurl in space a red-eyed star.—
For I'm told, beyond my curtain there revolveth day and night,
And among the stars there standeth one that winketh red with fight;
And you say the glow that lights upon my cheek is from the sun
Guiding lightning-footed planets as they in their orbits run;

And I've heard that all have sprung from atoms crowding God's abyss,—
Mars, the evil-eyed and warlike; Sol, the pivot-point of bliss.

### VII.

Yes, a weakness, sprung from weakness, weaker waxes, and a strength
On from strength to strength goes marching, grasping God's right hand at length;
For the mickle at the shoulder means the muckle at the hand,
And the hair's breadth on the compass means the ship upon the land.

### VIII.

Aye, wife; now I know the reason why you sighed so since we wed:
You have seen the world hang on you. Don't you mind, dear, what you read
Out of Cowper?—where he speaks of how the arrow on the wing
Falls at last far out of line though small the error at the string.

### IX.

There he's: take him! You can rhyme of chubby cheeks, and laughy eyes
That have housed far down within them little patches of the skies;

You can paint your glowing pictures, that a tear may wash away
When a future Vandal stumbles through your dream some after day.
Mine are coloured from th' eternal, set by Love in Fancy's mould,
Knowing nought of life's mutations, Summer's heat or Winter's cold.

### X.

So you've only come this morning, courier dove with pinions white?
What's the news from God, what message from the hidden heart of Night?

# Sundry Songs and Sonnets.

## The Southern Cross.

Afar from his wife and his sons and his daughters,
  The fisherman grapples for gain or loss ;
Beneath him the silent midnight waters ;
  Above him the blaze of the Southern Cross :
And ever his thoughts on the breeze hie homeward,
  As he calls to the watcher again and again,—
    "O what of the night : is it dark or bright ?"
  And ever there cometh the old refrain,—
    " The skies are clearing, the dawn is nearing,
    The midnight shadows fly.
    The Cross is bending, the night is ending,
    The day is drawing nigh."

Again, on the storm-swept winter waters,
  He battles the billows that tumble and toss ;
And he thinks of the weeping of wives and daughters,
  As the clouds fly over the Southern Cross.

Ah, then in the hour of his heart's despairing,
  When sheets are rending and cables strain,
    How sweet to his ear come the words of cheer,
  And the sound of the watcher's old refrain,—
    " The skies are clearing, the dawn is nearing,
    The midnight shadows fly.
    The Cross is bending, the night is ending,
    The day is drawing nigh."

.   .   .   .   .   .   .

Far out, far out on Life's wild waters,
  Where storms are howling, where breakers toss,
How many of earth's fair sons and daughters
  Are drifting and dragging to gain or loss !
But ever the Stars of Hope are shining,
  Through calm and tempest, through wind and rain ;
    And soft through the night, be it dark or bright,
  The heart still echoes the old refrain,—
    " The skies are clearing, the dawn is nearing,
    The midnight shadows fly.
    The Cross is bending, the night is ending.
    The day is drawing nigh."

# On the Death of William Morris.

### I.

Mine eyes beheld thee—but not nigh: mine ear,
  Close to thy page, could feel the beat, beat, beat,
  That told thy great, good heart: now strangers' feet
Have borne thee out. Thee? Nay, I have thee here
Forever young; nor less that eye, so clear,
  Beams brotherhood, nor can the years that fleet
  Leave me more lonely. No hot tear—full meet
From widowed Friendship—drop I on thy bier.
  Some earth-stained page mars oft fair Friend-ships's book;
And happier I, who saw thro' Fancy's light
  Kin only of the sacred singing race,
Blameless of all that mars familiar sight!—
  Then wherefore should I weep, who skyward look,
    And mark a god move Godward to his place?

## II.

Perfume of eld, more sweet than all the scent
   Of late-blown roses squandered on the air,
   Sweetens the tawny forest of thy hair,
And there shall dwell till all the years be spent.
To thee war's call with hint of song is blent,
   And time sits easy on the brows of care;
   Love lifts a white affirming hand to swear
Thee hero of thy heroes,—thou, who went
      To the frore Past. Lo! in its eyes did dance
   Reflection of a day within the wake
Of some unrisen, kindlier star; and thou
Didst cry: " Behold, with goodlier days the Now
   Is great, as forests wave in seeds to break,
      And countless thousands pulse in Love's
        first glance!"

# Copernicus.

They deemed, self-centred souls! that those great
   eyes
   Which star the night, in amorous orbit turned
   And, ever boldly bashful, sighed and burned
For one earth kiss, and stood within the skies
Eternally expectant.  O most wise
   In your great selves! that rude iconoclast
   His stones of Truth among your dreamings cast,
And robbed your wisdom of its dear disguise.
   He stood, a Sampson of Titanic force,
     'Twixt men and God, and swiftly grasped and
       hurled
His bolts at callow thoughts of centuries,
   And pivoted th' unreckoned universe,
     And marked the rhythmic orbit of a world,
And changed chaotic chords to harmonies!

# To Algernon Charles Swinburne.

(To remind him that the Genius of Ireland, nigh twenty centuries ago, taught the dull ears of the world the subtleties and charms of the rhyme of which he is now acknowledged master.)

Moulder of mighty measures and sublime ;
  Whose flower of song—how dead soe'er the ground—
    Blossoms : whose feet, from no great depth profound,
By cloudy slopes to cloudier summits climb !
What though thou art, in this thy world-broad prime,
  Great King of Song, sceptred and robed and crowned ;
    Be it not thine to scorn the narrow round
Whence broadened out the bounds of later time.
Not all the message of that far-off chime
  The strident strains of this our day have drowned :
"Forget not, Singer, whence hath sprung thy rhyme,
  Or whence thy tongue its lofty power hath found ;
Nor squander all thy store in mocking mime,
  Niggard of sense and prodigal of sound."

# Heaven and Earth.

*In the beginning the Heaven and the Earth were wedded together, and then was the golden age of joy and beauty. But something occurred which destroyed the union, and the Heaven and the Earth were parted amid the tears of Nature, which men call the dew.—*
LEGEND OF SOUTH SEA ISLANDS.

Truth in untruth ; wisdom on Folly's tongue,
   And substance in a shadow !—Hear ye this :
   Erewhile, 'mid transports of primeval bliss,
In starry ears a bridal song was sung,
And Heav'n and Earth, in mutual rapture, strung
   Ethereal harps, and took one reeling kiss,
   'Till, seated with much joy, Earth grew remiss:—
But, love was rife, and, ah! the Earth was young.

O trembling tears of dawn in Nature's eyes !
   Forget your sadness.  Lo ! methinks the hour
     When recreant Love turns loveward, thrills the dome ;
   Earth lifts mute praying hands in tree and flower,
And Heav'n, in all the windows of the skies,
     Hangs nightly lamps to light the wand'rer home !

# On Some Twentieth Century Forecasts.

O imperturable and silent years,
   That reck not all the riot of our time
   Whose fevered feet, with inharmonious rhyme,
Royster around thy high phantasmal tiers !
How mean our mockings of the silent seers
   To read the riddle of th' Eternal Soul !
   We list' the thundering life within thy bole,
And count the hidden harvest that anears,
   And dream our dreams, and smile to see them
      wrecked !
Oh, vain insurgence on the unrevealed :
   Enough to map the paths our fathers tracked ;
Not, mother-like, kiss yet the face concealed.
   Age ages not the elemental law,
And we are thou in hope, thou we anew,
   And still beneath are depths whence Shakspere
      drew,
   And still above are stars that Milton saw !

## Ireland.

Somewhat of Autumn's splendour round her lies ;
  Yet deem not thou 'tis preface of her death,
  For there is that within her heart which saith
This word that buds and blossoms in her eyes:—
" Reck not the portent of the season's skies,
  Nor deem yon darkling clouds aught but a breath
  Sundrawn from half a world that offereth
Its votive incense to the year that flies."
  The hand that bevels down the shortening day
Is one with that which quickens leaf and wing,
  So prophecy of pregnance in decay
Thou hast, and in thine Autumn germs of Spring ;
To vindicate these lips, that late have said :
" They dreamed a lie who deemed thee wholly dead ! "

www.ingramcontent.com/pod-product-compliance
Lightning Source LLC
Chambersburg PA
CBHW020309090426
42735CB00009B/1277